Beethoven

Alan Blackwood

Illustrated by Richard Hook

The Bookwright Press
New York · 1987

Great Lives

William Shakespeare
Elizabeth II
Anne Frank
Martin Luther King, Jr.
Helen Keller
Ferdinand Magellan
Mother Teresa
Louis Braille
John Lennon
John F. Kennedy

Florence Nightingale
Elvis Presley
Captain Cook
Gandhi
Napoleon
Einstein
Beethoven
Marie Curie
Elizabeth I
Karl Marx

First published in the
United States in 1987 by
The Bookwright Press
387 Park Avenue South
New York, NY 10016

First published in 1987 by
Wayland (Publishers) Ltd
61 Western Road, Hove
East Sussex, BN3 1JD, England

ISBN 0–531–18131–6
Library of Congress Catalog Card Number: 86–72827

Phototypeset by Kalligraphics Ltd, Redhill, Surrey
Printed in Italy by G. Canale & C.S.p.A., Turin

Contents

Young man at court

In 1770, Bonn, now the capital of West Germany, was a peaceful little town by the Rhine River. It was there on December 16, 1770, in a small room overlooking a backyard, that Ludwig van Beethoven was born. The Beethoven family, though German, came originally from the old Spanish Netherlands. Little Ludwig was called "der Spagnol" (the Spaniard) by friends and neighbors on account of his unusually dark, swarthy complexion. Perhaps he had some Spanish blood in his veins.

Ludwig's father, Johann, sang in the chapel and castle choir of the local Elector, or Count. Johann was a drunkard, who bullied his young son into playing the violin. "Scratch according to the notes!" he used to shout at the boy. Fortunately, there were other musicians in Bonn to whom Ludwig could turn. One was Christian Gottlob Neefe, an organist and composer who soon recognized that the boy was court. A family friend described him in his court uniform of "sea green tailcoat, flowered waistcoat, knee breeches with buckles, white silk stockings, black rosetted shoes, hat under his left arm, dagger at his side, and a pigtail of hair." This was the boy who was to become perhaps the greatest of all composers.

The pretty house where Beethoven lived in Bonn.

exceptionally gifted. He taught him musical theory and gave him encouragement, and told his friends about young Ludwig.

At the age of twelve, Ludwig was writing pieces for the piano. At thirteen he was a good enough musician to be appointed assistant organist at the Elector's

This statue of Beethoven in Bonn was erected to honor him.

City of music

Young Beethoven had many good friends in Bonn. One was Count Ferdinand Waldstein and another Frau von Breuning, who looked after him when his mother died, and encouraged his love of books and learning. When he was sixteen years old, they helped to arrange money for his first visit to Vienna, where many of Europe's finest musicians lived and worked. There he was introduced one day to Mozart, who heard him play the piano and declared, "Watch that boy! Some day he is going to make the world take notice of him!"

Back home in Bonn, Beethoven spent several years

Beethoven became an excellent pianist, admired by the Viennese.

playing the organ for the Elector, the violin in a local theater orchestra, and writing more music of his own. Then in 1792, Count Waldstein paid for him to return to Vienna, to study with Haydn, the most famous composer of the age.

Haydn taught Beethoven how to write music in what were the new classical forms and styles of the time – symphonies for the orchestra, string quartets, and sonatas for the piano. These were all types of composition containing three or four separate parts called movements and

Haydn (right) with his quartet. He taught Beethoven musical theory, but Beethoven found his views too traditional.

noted for the clear, orderly way they were put together and made to sound.

Beethoven, now in his early twenties, was a rebellious pupil. As soon as he had learned the rules about composing symphonies and sonatas, he wanted to change them. One teacher declared that Beethoven was too headstrong ever to learn anything! In a few more years, however, he was going to write music that would shake the world.

Beethoven and revolution

After Beethoven's studies with Haydn were completed, he stayed on in Vienna. He was a brilliant young pianist, especially good at improvising – making up music on the spur of the moment. He could rouse an audience to a great pitch of joyful excitement, or just as easily move them to tears with his playing.

Suddenly, he was being talked about by all the fashionable people of Vienna, and was invited to play for them in their homes. Aristocrats became his patrons, advancing him money and arranging concerts. Beethoven had first rented an attic room in the city. Soon he moved into the grand home of one of his patrons, Prince Carl Lichnowsky.

People were also fascinated by Beethoven's looks and manner.

Besides having a swarthy complexion, he was short and burly, with a very large head crowned with a shock of thick, black hair. Haydn, like any gentleman of his generation, always wore a wig in public. Beethoven never bothered with such a thing.

His behavior was even more remarkable. Almost all musicians and other artists before him, whether they were employed by a king or a prince or

The women of Paris on the march during the French Revolution, which inspired Beethoven.

by the Church, had been treated much like servants. But in 1789 the French Revolution had begun with calls for freedom and equality. Beethoven was excited and inspired by this event. Nobody was going to treat him like a servant. When another of his patrons, Prince Franz von Lobkowitz, annoyed him, he exclaimed "Lobkowitz is a donkey!" Haydn or Mozart would never have dared to behave like that.

A new Prometheus

One of Beethoven's early compositions was music for a ballet about Prometheus, a character in Greek mythology who stole fire from heaven and gave it to the human race. Beethoven thought of himself as a kind of Prometheus, bringing to music a depth of feeling and thought that no composer before him had done.

Many of his other early compositions were piano sonatas, which he composed for himself to play at concerts and recitals. One of them is called the Pathétique Sonata, meaning a sonata full of feeling. It has a wild and stormy opening movement, followed by a gentle slow movement, like a beautiful song. This was Beethoven bringing new fire and feeling to music.

Beethoven's attitude to his work as a composer was equally new. Most composers wrote music as their employers asked for it, usually for some special occasion, heard it performed once, and often forgot about it afterwards. Beethoven, by contrast, wrote most of his music as and when he wanted. He thought long and hard about each new composition, and refused to be hurried. And because he put so much effort into his music, he expected it to be performed not just once or twice, but many times, so that people could really understand it.

Sometimes Beethoven flew into a rage if other people criticized one of his pieces. But he was very critical of his own work. Only when he was really pleased with a new composition would he allow it to be published. The importance he attached to his work singled him out as an entirely new kind of creative artist.

An extract from a score written by Beethoven.

Right *Beethoven was often extremely critical of his own work.*

A terrible blow

Beethoven was tortured by noises in his ears.

In 1800, when he was thirty years old, Beethoven published his First Symphony. Mozart, at the same age, had written nearly forty symphonies. But for Beethoven a symphony was something very special, and he waited until he was sure he could write a good one. In the same year – the first of a new century – he composed his Moonlight sonata, a nickname afterwards given to it because someone said the dreamy, reflective first movement reminded him of moonlight. The rest of the sonata is not dreamy at all, but bright and cheerful, then fiery.

There is no hint in any of this music that something was going terribly wrong in Beethoven's life. He was suffering from

12

buzzing noises in his ears, and often he could not hear what people said to him. He realized he was going deaf. For a while he kept his trouble a secret from all but his closest friends and the doctors whom he consulted. But in 1802, when it seemed there was no cure for his condition, he poured out his agony of mind in a document called the Heiligenstadt Testament, written in the village of Heiligenstadt, not far from Vienna. Addressing himself to the world at large, he confessed, "I could not bring myself to say to people 'Speak louder, shout, for I am deaf.' How should I bring myself to admit the weakness of a sense that ought to be more perfect in me than in others. Forgive me, if you see me shrinking away when I would fain mingle with you."

The Heiligenstadt Testament was also a kind of will. For in his misery and distress, Beethoven was sure he was soon to die.

The entrance to Beethoven's house at Heiligenstadt, just outside Vienna.

The heroic symphony

Beethoven did not die. He began instead to compose some of his greatest music.

He was, as we have read, inspired by the French Revolution. He also admired Napoleon Bonaparte for defeating France's enemies and creating a new kind of society in Europe. So he at first dedicated his Third Symphony to Napoleon. Then, in 1804, Beethoven heard that Napoleon had crowned himself Emperor of the French. He angrily scratched out the dedication to Napoleon on the title page of the manuscript

Beethoven was furious when he heard Napoleon had crowned himself Emperor of France.

The house in Döbling where Beethoven composed the Eroica Symphony.

score. By taking a crown, so Beethoven argued, Napoleon had betrayed the movement for freedom and equality. Instead, he called his new symphony the Eroica, or (heroic) Symphony.

Beethoven is the real hero of the music. His growing deafness had ruined his career as a pianist. But he refused to be beaten. Though he could not hear accurately the sounds that reached his ears, he could still "hear" music in his mind. So he put all his efforts into composition, and his music grew even more magnificient.

The Eroica Symphony left its first audience amazed and almost speechless, both by the huge scale on which it was planned, and by the immense power of the music itself. The second movement is a funeral march that begins quietly and solemnly, then rises to a tremendous climax. The symphony ends with a set of variations – a type of musical composition that keeps presenting the same basic theme or melody in different ways. Beethoven based these variations on a theme from his earlier Prometheus ballet music. They are a marvelous example of how he could create so much great music from one simple little dance tune.

A new kind of opera

Beethoven's deafness often made him bad tempered and difficult to get along with, but Prince Lobkowitz and his other patrons stood by him. Publishers, too, were eager to print and sell his music, even though much of it seemed to them strange and difficult. Beethoven was famous. But he also wanted to become a more popular composer, by writing an opera. In those days, far more people went to the theater to hear and see operas than had the chance to listen to a symphony or a string quartet.

Beethoven chose as the subject for his opera the story of a man who has been wrongfully imprisoned and sentenced to death. His faithful wife disguises herself as a man, gains entry into the prison and rescues him just as he is to be taken out and shot.

Beethoven liked the plot because he took very seriously his beliefs in individual freedom and the power of love. But the opera was at first a failure. People wanted operas with catchy tunes or lots of spectacle, and they didn't much enjoy one set for long stretches in a gloomy prison. It was only after Beethoven had revised and shortened his opera, and changed its title from *Leonore* (the name of the heroine) to *Fidelio* (meaning faithful), that audiences began to appreciate its wonderful depth of feeling.

As a result of all Beethoven's revisions, there were several Leonore Overtures. Overtures are played by the orchestra before the actual opera begins. Today they are often played on their own, in concerts. They are almost like different versions of the same piece, and show us how ideas grew in Beethoven's mind, to be translated into music of towering strength and power.

The audiences didn't like an opera mainly set in a prison.

Victory and peace

While he was revising his opera *Fidelio*, Beethoven also composed his Fifth Symphony. Almost everybody knows its famous opening, which some call the "fate" theme, and others think stands for "victory," because its rhythm is the same as the morse code "V" for victory. This mighty symphony also set the pattern for many other symphonies in the way it suggests a kind of struggle, from its tense and dramatic start toward a final mood of triumph. Beethoven certainly struggled hard to compose it.

He found his sixth symphony an easier task. This is the Pastoral Symphony, and conveys the composer's love of the countryside. Beethoven

Beethoven loved the countryside.

frequently took holidays in the villages around Vienna and went for long walks, when new musical ideas came to him in the peace and quiet of woods and fields. He always took with him a notebook, or sketchbook, in which he jotted down such ideas. Scholars have studied these sketchbooks, to see how Beethoven painstakingly worked on his ideas, gradually changing them (much like a sculptor chipping away at stone), until they were ready to fit into

The famous Vienna State Opera House, where Fidelio is performed today.

the larger scheme of a composition.

The Pastoral Symphony is quiet and gentle compared with the Fifth Symphony, but it is also a revolutionary work. It is program music in the way it paints in sound such scenes as a babbling brook, peasants dancing, or the sun shining after a thunderstorm. There are even imitation bird calls. No one before Beethoven had thought of doing anything like it in a symphony. It is a big stepping stone between the classical music of Haydn and Mozart and the romantic, descriptive music of later composers, such as Berlioz, Schumann and Liszt.

Emperor Concerto

In 1809 the paths of Beethoven and Napoleon nearly crossed. Napoleon attacked and occupied Vienna, setting up his headquarters in the royal palace of Schönbrunn, just outside the city. Beethoven, for his part, had to take refuge in a cellar, holding cushions to his head to protect his ears from the noise of Napoleon's guns.

He was working at the time on another masterpiece, the Fifth Piano Concerto. This is known as the "Emperor" Concerto, although it was not named after Napoleon. It is, however, quite a good name for the work – the last and grandest of Beethoven's concertos, composed at the height of the Napoleonic Wars. Whether or not the bombardment of Vienna had anything directly to do with it, there are moments in the music when we could well imagine a brave cavalry charge,

Left *Beethoven sat in his cellar protecting his ears from the gunfire.*

Right *Napoleon set up headquarters at the Schönbrunn Palace.*

with a gleam of helmets and flash of swords, or the roar and smoke of a cannonade.

The Emperor Concerto is also a landmark in Beethoven's creative thinking. In all concertos before this one, composers left gaps in the music, which were supposed to be filled by special displays of playing by the soloist. Such passages of solo playing are called cadenzas. But in his Emperor Concerto, Beethoven ties together the music for the orchestra and the solo piano so closely that there is no place for an old-fashioned cadenza. By composing the entire concerto from start to finish, Beethoven was making the point that he didn't want anybody else interfering with his music! This was one of the ways in which he raised the status of the composer from that of servant to master.

Beethoven hated the entry of Napoleon and the French into Vienna, in 1805.

The immortal beloved

"My thoughts turn to you, my immortal beloved, some of them happy, some sad, waiting to see whether fate will hear us. I can live only completely with you or not at all . . ."

So reads part of a love letter found in Beethoven's desk after his death. Who was the "immortal beloved"? Was it Theresa, Countess von Brunswick, or one of the other fashionable women who came to Beethoven for piano lessons? Nobody knows.

Beethoven had many love affairs, and he wanted to get married, but the women he fell in

Was the love letter Beethoven wrote to Theresa, Countess von Brunswick?

love with were nearly all titled ladies, members of Viennese high society. They were attracted to the famous composer but were not prepared to marry him. Some were married already.

So Beethoven remained a bachelor. He changed residence frequently, and as he grew older cared for himself less and less. Sometimes a manservant looked

Beethoven conducting a quartet, surrounded by admirers.

after him, but sooner or later Beethoven would lose his temper, and the servant would leave. Friends and patrons helped as much as they could, but the composer refused assistance.

"Imagine the dirtiest and most disorderly room possible," wrote one friend who had visited him about the year 1810. "There was water on the floor, a rather ancient piano covered with dust and paper. Next to it was a small table stained with spilled ink. The chairs were covered with clothes, and there were dishes with the remains of last night's supper."

There are many such descriptions of Beethoven's sad and lonely home life.

Beethoven ceased to care for himself. He was often bad tempered with servants.

Drunk with genius

As Beethoven's deafness increased, he had to use hearing aids – specially shaped trumpets he held up to his ears – and had "conversation books," in which people wrote down questions for him to read and answer.

But, like all great artists, Beethoven forgot about everything else when he was working, and his music often bears little relation to the growing sadness of his life. The seventh and eighth symphonies were composed about 1812 – the year of Napoleon's invasion of Russia and terrible winter retreat from Moscow, and both are wonderful expressions of joy and humor. On first hearing the wild and joyful dance of the Seventh Symphony's last movement, one listener declared that the composer must have been drunk when he wrote it. "Yes, drunk with genius!" replied another, who understood the music better.

Beethoven could also write music full of fun. When he was in a relaxed, happy mood, he would sometimes creep up on friends and slap them hard on the back, or come in out of the rain and shake the water out of his coat all over them, laughing loudly as he did so. The Eighth Symphony shows this boisterous side of his character. Its second movement has an added point of interest. One of Beethoven's friends, Johann Maelzel, had just devised a metronome – a clockwork instrument with a loud, regular click, intended to help musicians keep to the beat of a piece of music. The Eighth Symphony's

second movement is a comic imitation of Maelzel's ticking metronome, even to the point where it starts to slow down and has to be wound up again!

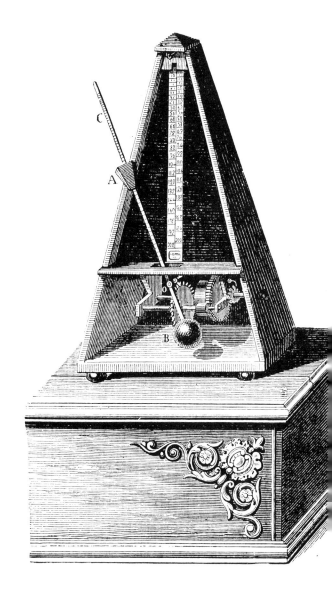

Beethoven's Eighth Symphony imitated the metronome, a new device.

Ode to Joy

Around 1815, the time of the Battle of Waterloo, Beethoven was involved in a long family quarrel and expensive court case in order to become the legal guardian of his nephew Karl, of whom he was very fond. It was a miserable time for the composer, but when it was over he worked harder than ever.

One of his new compositions was the Hammerklavier Sonata, which he said should be played on the very lastest type of hammerklavier or piano. In fact, proper performances of this giant sonata had to wait for many years, until even bigger and stronger pianos were made.

Beethoven also worked on a huge church mass (the Missa Solemnis or solemn mass) for another of his patrons, the Archduke Rudolph of Austria, and also on his ninth (or Choral) symphony. The Choral Symphony had an orchestra twice as large as that required by any earlier symphony, plus solo singers and

When Beethoven faced the audience, he saw them applauding.

Beethoven's famous broadwood piano, which he used when composing.

a big chorus. Beethoven filled it with more music of tremendous power. It ends with a setting for the singers and orchestra of a poem called "Ode to Joy," proclaiming men and women of all races as brothers and sisters. This triumphant, march-like chorus, which Beethoven had been thinking about for many years, made the music reach out to express the highest hopes of people everywhere.

At the first performance of the Choral Symphony in 1824, the orchestra and chorus made many mistakes, because they had never before tackled music anything like it. But at the end the deaf composer, who had been trying to follow the performance up on the stage, turned around to face the audience rising to their feet to acclaim him.

Defiant to the last

Beethoven was a tough man, but the enormous effort he had put into his work for years on end finally made him ill, as well as deaf. Despite everything, when he felt strong enough he went on working, composing a last group of string quartets, which some people consider his very finest works. A movement from one of them is called "Holy Song of Thanksgiving by One Recovered from Sickness." He started to plan a Tenth Symphony.

Before dying, Beethoven shook his fist defiantly at the thunder.

Beethoven's monument looks down on a market square in Vienna, the city where he died.

Alas, Beethoven was soon seriously ill again, and in March 1827 he lapsed into a coma. Doctors and friends crowded into his small, untidy room. Several of them recorded that on the 26th of that month there was a sudden flash of lightning and a loud clap of thunder, at which the composer opened his eyes and shook his fist at the window, defiant to the last. Minutes later he died. He was fifty-six.

Beethoven had lived alone for most of his life, but thousands of people joined his funeral procession through Vienna. They may not have heard much of his music, nor clearly understood it. But they knew a great man had died. Indeed, the power and expressiveness of Beethoven's music influenced nearly every other great composer for the next hundred years. It has also stirred the hearts and minds of millions, as no other music had done.

29

Dates and events

1770   Ludwig van Beethoven born in Bonn.

1783   Appointed organist at the court of the Elector of Bonn.

1789   The start of the French Revolution.

1792   Settles in Vienna and studies music, as Haydn's pupil.

1798–9   First group of important compositions, including Pathétique Sonata, and first two piano concertos.

1800–1   Symphony No 1, six string quartets, Moonlight Sonata.

1802   Confesses to deafness in Heiligenstadt Testament. Symphony No 2, Piano Concerto No 3.

1803–4   Symphony No 3 (Eroica), Appassionata Sonata.

1805–7   Piano Concerto No 4, Violin Concerto, "Rassumovsky" string quartets, Symphony No 4, Symphony No 5, first version of opera *Fidelio*.

1808–9   Suffers during Napoleon's bombardment of Vienna. Symphony No 6 (Pastoral), Piano Concerto No 5 (Emperor).

1810–12   Deafness increasing. Music to Goethe's play *Egmont*, Symphony No 7, Symphony No 8.

1815–18   Goes to court over family quarrel about the custody of his young nephew Karl.

1819–23   "Hammerklavier" Sonata, Mass in D (Missa Solemnis), Symphony No 9 (Choral Symphony).

1824   First performance of Choral Symphony. Starts work on new group of string quartets.

1825–6   Falls ill, but completes his last five string quartets.

1827   Final illness, and death in Vienna, March 26. Thousands join his funeral procession.

The dates of Beethoven's compositions are only approximate, as he worked on some of them for years.

Glossary

Cadenza   A place in a concerto where solists play on their own.

Classical music   Stricly speaking, music composed between about 1750 and 1800, in the style of symphonies, string quartets, sonatas, and following special rules about how the music should be put together.

Concerto   A composition for one or more solosits and an orchestra. An Italian word meaning "play together."

Opera   Combination of music and drama.

Orchestra   Group of musicians playing a variety of instruments. During Beethoven's lifetime orchestras grew in size from about thirty to seventy players. Modern orchestras often have over a hundred players.

Overture   Orchestral piece, often played at the start of an opera, though some composers have written overtures as pieces on their own.

Program music   Music that is meant to evoke a particular scene or event; a kind of musical painting.

Romantic music   Most music written between about 1800 and 1900, when composers cared less about rules and more about the mood or feeling of their music.

Score   The written or printed version of a piece of music.

Sonata   Composition, for solo piano, or for piano and one other instrument, usually in several separate pieces, or "movements." From the Italian *suonare*, "to sound."

String quartet   Type of chamber music, usually for two violins, one viola and a cello, rather like a small symphony.

Symphony   Orchestral composition, sometimes with a chorus, usually in several separate pieces, or "movements." From the Greek word meaning "harmonious."

Books to Read

Beethoven, by David Jacobs. Harper and Row Juvenile Books, 1970.

A Book of Great Composers: Book 1, by David Brownell. Bellerphon Books, 1978.

A Concise History of Music, by Percy M. Young. David White Co., 1973.

Heroes and Heroines in Music, by Wendy-Ann Ensor. Oxford University Press, 1981. (cassette available)

More Stories of Composers for Young Musicians, by Catherine W. Kendall. Toadwood, 1985.

The Value of Giving: The Story of Beethoven, by Ann D. Johnson. Value Communications, 1979.

Index